Peppa Pig™

Daddy Pig's Lost Keys

Peppa and her family are on a day trip, visiting the mountains. It's time to go back to the car.

"Thank you for visiting the mountain beauty spot," says Miss Rabbit.

"Key! Key!" snorts George.
"You can't play with the car keys!"
laughs Daddy Pig. "You might lose them."

Daddy Pig *can*
play with the
car keys because
he's a grown-up.

"Whoops!"
Oh dear. Daddy Pig
has dropped the car
keys down a drain.

"Time to go home!" says Mummy Pig. Daddy Pig goes red. "That might be difficult," he says.

Daddy Pig tries to get
the keys out of the drain
with a stick.
"Hmm . . ." he says.
"The drain is deeper than
I thought."

The drain is very deep.
The stick is not long
enough to reach the keys.

Hmmm...

Daddy Pig has a better idea.
"What we need is a fishing rod!"
So he buys one from
Miss Rabbit.

Daddy Pig's idea doesn't work. The fishing line is not long enough to reach the keys.

Mr Bull and his friends arrive.
They've come to enjoy the quiet beauty spot.
"It's our day off!" shouts Mr Bull.
Mr Bull talks very loudly.

"Er, Mr Bull?" asks Daddy Pig. "Could we borrow your crane for a minute to rescue my keys?"

"Say no more," cries Mr Bull. "We'll have your keys out in no time!"

Mr Rhino gets to work,
but it's no good. Even
the crane can't reach
the keys!

"Easy!" shouts Mr Bull.
"We'll dig up the road!"

The crew dig up the beauty spot.
Mr Bull is lowered all the way down
to the bottom of the hole.
"Here are the keys!" he bellows.
"We've got them!"

Now there is a big hole in the mountain beauty spot.
It is a cave beauty spot instead.
"And it's all thanks to my daddy!" giggles Peppa.

Ooh!

Yay!